Aeolian Harp
volume 7

Edited by Megan Merchant & Ami Kaye

Guest Editor: Megan Merchant
Series Editor: Ami Kaye
Project Manager: Royce Ellen Hamel
Layout, Book & Cover Design: Steven M. Asmussen
Copyediting: Linda Kim
Cover Artist: Tracy McQueen

Fonts "National Oldstyle", "Persnickety", and "Metro Thin" designed by
Andrew Leman, courtesy of The H. P. Lovecraft Historical Society, www.cthulhulives.org

Aeolian Harp Series: Anthology of Poetry Folios
Volume 7, First Printing
Copyright © 2021 Glass Lyre Press, LLC
Paperback ISBN: 978-1-941783-81-8

All rights reserved: Except for the purpose of quoting brief passages for review, no part of this book may be reproduced or transmitted in any form or by any means, electronic or mechanical, including photocopying, recording, or by any information storage and retrieval system, without permission in writing from the publisher.

Glass Lyre Press, LLC
P.O. Box 2693
Glenview, IL 60025

www.GlassLyrePress.com

Foreword

Megan Merchant, Guest Editor

I'm not going to lie, when I began reading the submissions for this anthology, I had to look up the history of the aeolian harp. I discovered that it is "a box shaped musical instrument having stretched strings usually tuned in unison on which the wind produces various harmonies over the same fundamental tone" (Merriam-Webster). Given this, I decided to read each entry outside. I read in the sun, listening for their sounds caught in the wind, looking for the fundamental connection between poems, between moments, and between writers. I found their very landscapes, perspectives, histories, and hearts stretched over one common theme—what it means to be human in this world. And while each folio is rooted in different mechanisms—rich imagery, narrative, sound play, and/or lyricism, to express this—that common theme is present and pulsing in each one. As Adrienne Rich said, "We go to poetry because we believe it has something to do with us. We also go to poetry to receive the experience of the not me, enter a field of vision we could not otherwise apprehend." In this way, we can build empathy. In holding the perspective, voice, and experience of another in our minds, we can expand.

I was grateful for that expansion, for the opportunity to enter new fields of vision, because over the past year, like many others, mine has been stifled by the pandemic blues—disconnection, loss of touch, and cinched glimpses of life outside of these walls. So, the chance to enter the worlds that each poet creates and strings together across multiple pages, for more than a soundbite, truly helped me to remember that poetry is not just well-crafted language on a page—it sings, it heals, it awakens, it teaches, and it helps us to erase the outlines of otherness that can so easily be mistaken as solid, especially when we are isolated from each other.

I hope that these pages, landscapes, images and words unfold both a familiar and new understanding for you, reader, about what it means to be human in this world. I hope, that if you listen closely, you will be able to catch the harmony in the wind.

Megan Merchant
Guest Editor, AHS

...this harp which I wake now for thee
    Was a siren of old who sung under the sea.

— Thomas Moore, *The Origin of the Harp*

Folios

Scott Ferry	1
Kari Gunter-Seymour	13
Michael Meyerhofer	23
Connie Post	35
Kimberly Ann Priest	47
Lindsey Royce	55
Barbara Ungar	67
Alexandrine Vo	77
Jeanne Wagner	91
Martin Willitts Jr.	103

Scott Ferry

When I was a sophomore in high school I used to wring my hands over my writing. Every word was rusty and awkward and ill-placed. When I started writing poems quite spontaneously for no apparent reason, all of that changed. I found flow from somewhere and writing became less tortuous. For me, it has always been about getting out of the way, killing the Buddha on the path, turning off the viewfinder so I can destroy the Death Star by feel. Every single time I try to over-edit any piece of writing, or edit it while it is coming out, it dries up on me. And, the exasperating part of my process is that if I don't have enough time or quiet or space to finish the poem in one go, it will drift off. Sure, I can try to finish it later, but it doesn't keep that thread on the needle to the end. I want a feeling of rushing water when I am done, a velocity through the stanzas which feels natural and whole. Not that I always achieve this by a long shot, but this is what I try to do—to allow it to all come out at once.

A few months ago I posted a question on Facebook to the effect of "Do you give some credit to the muse for your art?" The response was overwhelming yes from most poets. So I have to give credit to the ghostly voice which prods me to write this down, even throws words into my head that I have to look up. Just recently, I was given "immutable malleability" through the ether for one of my poems. Who says that? The guy who drives his fleshy self to work and struggles to make small talk certainly doesn't. So, I have learned to listen and to be available when a poem twitches yellow-winged in my periphery. I will email myself a key word so I can give myself to it later. Then I do very little to steer it. And, I guess if I keep listening, they will keep coming.

Box

story by my daughter Leilani for a 2nd grade assignment

a box of gold   and diamonds
arrives at   my front door
when I open it   blue light

turns me into an   anime cat girl
a smaller box   appears
in its place made   of sapphire

and inside it   glows a lapis
necklace   with thin bands
streaked like   wind

I lift it and it   flies around
my neck   becoming a choker
I see a note   from my great

great great great   grandmother
(and I can hear   her whisper
as I read   the words)

I have passed   this down
from mother   to daughter
and now to you   so you too

will hold the power   of the wind.
And then the box   swirls into
the air   indigo and white

sparks go into   the necklace
and into my skin   and I feel
the wind   within me

rise

After I Find My Daughter's Betta Dead

bleached and silver on the turquoise
rocks she begins to stick pearls
into the dark openings
begins to describe how a body

without a soul is first a monster
then a wind without ribs
then just a body
and the other parts are flying

without the bones or face
just the light in the air
and she can hear
gills near her ear

the fish says good things
and mean things
he was scared
because he couldn't see

and kept spitting out his food
even after the medicine
we gave him for weeks
he knew we tried to save him

but he was scared
and then he couldn't breathe
and fell upside down
mouth gulping

until his body stopped
and a young silver fish
flipped his tail through the glass
now seeing all the bright

water

Don/Doff

We are mandated to go to PPE training
where we prepare for all the infected patients
who will blister from the walls of this hospital—
fluid-filled and pale.

The instructor exudes calm professionalism
as we watch a video on how to scour our hands:
wring fists together like two sumo wrestlers,
twist around the trunk of each thumb,
steeple up the empty roofs and quake,
pinch the digits together, and rub
on the palms as if starting a fire.

Then we go to an imaginary droplet
room in which a person (our neighbor
our friend our grandmother) is drowning.
I volunteer and attempt to joke
"Oh great, I got the hardest scenario!"
and everyone returns a magnetic hostility.
The teacher retorts "This is actually the easiest one."

Don: gown, tie behind back, mask N95. Wait—
wash hands: squeeze/tree/church/clutch/burn.
Gloves up over cuffs. Face shield with plastic
barrier over eyes. Enter room facing the ill.
Do patient care (as if that was the easiest part).
Back away from the contaminated area.
Wash gloved hands: wrest/whorl/spire/pinch/flame.
Wipe the doorknob and threshold. Keep your dirty
face toward the body (remember: dirty to dirty).
Exit the door.

Doff: gown, like pulling off charred skin.
Roll it up into a wet heart.
Pull soiled gloves over and discard.
Wash hands: crush/circle/tent/curl/excoriate.
Doff outer mask. Keep facing the door.
(Dirty to dirty.) Make sure your eyes are dry
before removing your inner mask.

Unbody

1.   electrical coils scratch sinuses
a limped boot scrapes cement (don't sneeze)
my clothes almost touch the sparks as i hide

2.   joshua trees and yucca stream by the train
there is no train yet the camera and body
lift and follow as i grip my mother's purse

3.   brain corals and octopi wall the room
my interview can't be here and regardless
my résumé blurs at this depth

4.   i see her coffee areola but she can't hear me
as she touches my wrist she screams
i have always been scaled armless hissing

5.   she is the tallest in line as lights waver
she boards the plane and i don't kiss her neck—
our future children unbody like sulfur in their beds

Eviction

my father's ghost lived
in his beloved mammoth mt. condo for years

one tenant i found didn't pay rent
blew tobacco and had a dog

he never cleaned and i attempted to evict him
phoned his mother to get money

one night the other roommates woke up at 3 am
to steps and deliberate clanking of ceramic

and when they turned on the light—
dishes stacked in exact piles

even pots and pans fitted inside each other's
aluminum skins but they were the only ones there

the smoking renter still out drinking
they called me the next day

said everything looked ready to be placed
into boxes

my sister and i decided my father either
wanted him to move out or was packing his

brown-green 1970s plates for a move
from this state to the next

he died so suddenly after his retirement
he never got to ski again like he was 20

single drinking until 3
he wasn't about to let someone else

inhabit his lost skin

Streetlights

The woman I dated when I was 27
used to explain that her father communicated
with her through streetlights, hallway lights,
electrical appliances of all types.
He committed suicide three years before.
I lost my father about the same time
so we navigated these dimly lit roads
together. We would be driving
in Long Beach, where all the lights
are tinged bitter orange,
and she would snap her head
towards a light that extinguished right
before we passed, then I would feel
her soften, sadden, close her
eyes with a secret grin,
reaching through the fabric
of night to hold one darkened
hand.

Kari Gunter-Seymour

I am a ninth generation Appalachian. For well over a century, Appalachians have been marginalized and stereotyped. This deliberate ploy has affected multiple generations and was intended to dehumanize and belittle so that major U.S. coal companies could gain access to Appalachia's immense coal reserves. Appalachians began to be characterized as barefoot, overfed, undereducated and undergroomed and the land was consumed by coal removal. When Appalachians are portrayed as white trash, it is easier to pull off the ruse that coal companies were/are in the business to save Appalachia, rather than plunder.

My father's people left Berkshire England in the early 1700's and settled in Henrico county, Virginia. My great, great, great, great grandparents helped found and settle Aiken, SC. My mother's great grandfather came to this country from Belfast, Northern Ireland to settle in Mason, WV. I grew up not a mile from my grandparent's farm in southeastern Ohio. For many generations, my people were successful farmers. They took pride in their work ethic and lifestyle. They were not ashamed of the way they dressed or talked or what they chose to talk about. They were highly respected in the community for their knowledge of cultivation and husbandry. Today, Appalachia is teaming with bright, talented individuals who are skilled, well educated, and proudly tied to their Appalachian roots.

Like my people before me, my work is firmly and unapologetically attached to my home soil. More than merely commenting, I search for meaning. I take readers outside and indoors, into the world and into bodies and minds, a foray into the tangled bonds of family, weighted with memories. My poems speak to a knowing that as the threads of our lives unravel, so too, gifts materialize. There is specific cultural musicality of language and a strong sense of observation inviting readers to consider that preconceived prejudices need no longer be the gauge by which society judges Appalachians.

There have been many things written about how dreadful Appalachia is. I am always pleased for the opportunity to offer a different perspective, highlighting the spirituality and perseverance of my people and the beauty, honor and pride embedded in our culture.

I Come From A Place So Deep Inside America It Can't Be Seen

White oaks thrash, moonlight drifts
the ceiling, as if I'm under water.
Propane coils, warms my bones.

Gone are the magics and songs,
all the things our grandmothers buried–
piles of feathers and angel bones,

inscribed by all who came before.
When I was twelve, my cousins
called me ugly, enough to make it last.

Tonight a celebrity on Oprah
imagines a future where features
can be removed and replaced

on a whim. A moth presses wings
thin as paper against my window,
more beautiful than I could ever be.

Ryegrass raise seedy heads
beyond the bull thistle and preen.
Everything alive aches for more.

To No One In Particular

I am never happy to see summer go,
earth stripped of its finest voice.
I am sitting outside in my heavy coat,
porch light off. There is no moon,
no ambient distractions, the sky a Zion.

I take solace in considering the age
of this valley, the way water
left its mark on Appalachia,
long before Peabody sunk a shaft,
Chevron augured the shale or ODOT
dynamited roadways through steep rock.

I grew up in a house where canned
fruit cocktail was considered a treat.
My sister and I fought over who got
to eat the fake cherries, standouts in the can,
though tasting exactly like every other
tired piece of fruit floating in the heavy syrup.

But it was store-bought, like city folks
and we were too gullible to understand
the corruption in the concept, our mother's
home-canned harvests superior in every way.
I cringe when I think of how we shamed her.

So much here depends upon
a green corn stalk, a patched barn roof,
weather, the Lord, community.
We've rarely been offered a hand
that didn't destroy.

Inside the house the lightbulb comes on
when the refrigerator door is opened.
My husband rummages a snack,
plops beside me on the porch to wolf it down,
turns, plants a kiss, leans back in his chair,
says to no one in particular,
A person could spend a lifetime
under a sky such as this.

Hooper Ridge Girl

There was the rain and your knotted hair,
unruly in that mountain wind. Wild-eyed
finches swung on Hollyhock spines
along the banks of Sunday Creek.

We wished for wings at our feet to carry us
over the dark surface, looked for signs
between clouds and the higher skies. Now,
not far from that scattered ridge, you lie

with the wind and water, where the odor
of dirt and grass and moldering
blossoms ploughed you under,
where once we cut across

our hands, pressed them together.
Me plain as a sip of water.
You more beauty than could be held
in something as soft as a body.

I Spoke To You Of Stars Instead

Against the night sky, it's hard
to tell stars from planets. In rooms
with old paint and small heaters,
you covered your head.

I wrapped the quilts tighter, imagined
myself a good mother, wore the deception
like a pair of hand-me-down shoes
rubbing my heels raw.

I still hear you kicking the ball.
I smell the lilac musty after rain.
Remember? I used to hold you
as you recited stories of waggery and grit.

Go ahead, count my every blink.
Say the words we can never take back.

This wringing of hands and dirty washrags,
your eyes two black holes. Me standing here
moonlighting, like it's my favorite way
to get through life.

Bethal Ridge Cemetery

On the edge that time thins, I stood
with aching arms, in a wrinkled dress.
Among the stones a holier-than-thou,
dark-robed and flailing,
recited psalms by the shovelful.

It's the body that feels pain,
but the brain delivers it.
To this day, sometimes driving
I see black wings flapping between
bare branches and overreact.

Someone once told me we make
everyone in our dreams into another
version of ourselves, that rage isn't rage
but sorrow turned back on itself,
the shape made of regret.

There must have been birds,
the noon-time smell of grass.
I can't say. Feathered arias
and earthy balms are not meant for
a woman with a fist in each pocket.

Hold Fast

The meeting ends with a prayer,
Hold fast the hand next to you.
Yesterday is a dream,
every tomorrow a vision of hope.
I squeeze the hands I hold,
a woman on either side,
one dressed in county-jail orange.
It's humbling. We are all struggling.

    My mother is perched and pillowed, dying,
    her mind a highway of eroding neural paths.
    She tells me intimate stories
    without knowing who I am, dramas
    whispering themselves into her ears.
    A road map of saga, left to me to sort.

The woman on my right notices the scar
in my palm, caught on a piece of barbed wire
when I hopped a fence with Mark Fouty,
sophomore year, somewhere near Torch, Ohio.
He took me sky diving, made his own beer,
gave me an engagement ring the summer of '78.
Tempting, but as my mom pointed out,
I was just beginning my life.

    My mother didn't have choices,
    having fled farm and family.
    My daddy fresh from the war,
    metaled and wired, a great catch,
    both of them so broken.
    On my sixteenth birthday I told her, I hate you.
    Now she says she hates to leave me.

Thomas Merton wrote,
If the world were to end tomorrow,
I would still plant a tree today.
I leave the meeting.
Drink black coffee from a plastic mug.
Listen to the in-betweens my mother spins.
Trace the ruthless shadows of December's moon.

Michael Meyerhofer

Often when I write, I imagine that my audience is the farm kids and factory workers I grew up with, with their empty pockets and big hearts hardened by pesticides and conspiracy theories. Is there a way to tell the stories I want to tell without coming across as pretentious? Likewise, am I honoring my subject matter through craft whilst avoiding the pit-traps of cliché and vapid oversimplification? For me, it's a study in contradiction, an attempt at balance, a mix between the primal and the elevated. Put enough way, I think there's a very real sense in which the crispness of the stars depends upon the existence of genocides and clogged toilets. The better you get at acknowledging injustice, the easier it is to recognize courage and mercy. A good poem pulls you in different directions the way a Zen koan does, and by doing so, it gives us floundering primates some sense of what we sense but cannot express. That's the hope, anyway. As with most things, I'm hoping that effort and intention go a long way in mitigating failure.

For Ahmaud Arbery, An Unarmed Black Jogger Killed For Allegedly Looking In The Window Of A House Under Construction

I was twenty-two, white, in love
that day I wasn't shot for trespassing.

It happened nearly two decades ago.
We started out in the backseat

of her parents' oxblood Subaru,
heading back from the country club

with bellies full of prime rib
and vegetables I could not name.

Then her father touched the brake,
pointed to a mansion being built

beyond a phalanx of dogwoods,
timbers stacked like wine-washed

bones on a generous plot of Iowa soil.
The crews had already gone home,

just some golden tape left behind.
So we pulled over, got out, explored—

her father darkly pinstriped, her mother
sporting a heavy rosary of pearls.

Before long, neighbors spotted us
and waved, smiling from their hoses.

Unfazed, my girlfriend and I
slipped away and touched primally

in what might have been a stranger's
future bedroom, its walls unmade.

After a great while, we reunited
beside half a staircase. Her parents

forgave our absence with a shrug
and the suggestion of frozen yogurt.

On the way back, I could smell her
on my fingers, which made her blush.

Meanwhile, her parents shared
daydreams of their own mansion

with taller floors and windows,
thicker drapes to block the sunset.

Urban Legend

My father sat me down to tell me
not about the secret powers of women
nor my mother's failing kidneys

but a story he'd just heard: a boy my age
vacationing with family in Mexico,
a boy who saw his kid-sister abducted

and gave chase through a throng
of brown bodies. How the parents,
when they noticed the absence,

sought the help of border guards
with eagles on their sleeves—
strong, faceless men who knew

it was already too late. An hour later,
the kids turned up with their guts
scooped out, replaced with narcotics

the cartel tried to smuggle across
a border bristling with rifles and flags.
In real life, I didn't have a sister

and we never vacationed anywhere
that took more than an hour to reach.
Still, I worried myself sick

imagining pills, powder, plants,
that tug-o-war on my insides,
wondered whether those bags of sin

lied flat like deflated balloons
or bulged like the moony breasts
of women I saw in magazines,

women with eyes like damp gravestones
who leaned on men with muscles
that spoke their own language.

A Belated Apology
To A Transgender Colleague

I still regret the time I high-fived a guy
who was halfway through
physically becoming a woman
and even said something terribly
heteromasculine like *Right on, dude!*
in answer to her praise
of a book we both loved. I meant it
to sound friendly and supportive,
so secure in my Midwestern liberality
that I almost missed the hesitation
in her eyes before she returned
the gesture—our bare palms
touching like shadows, the digits mirrored—
not to mention the scowls
of other colleagues at the table.
Then, a month later, attending a gala
alongside her and her wife, I walked up
and said, *Hello, ladies,*
thinking that would absolve me,
though even in my ears the words
sounded off kilter, due not
to insincerity but nerves, my own inability
to stand anyone thinking badly of me.
True, this isn't about my own
rotten childhood, but I seem
unable to speak as anybody but myself.
There's one other moment I return to:
walking by her office a few days
after my latest verbal idiocy
to ask how she'd been. She mentioned
a forthcoming operation, a little
catch in her voice, and in my haste
to commiserate, I said, *Oh, I have one of those*

coming up, too, merely referring
to a bit of dental work,
though her eyes widened
a split second before she said,
Well, man, good luck, and meant it.

My Mother's Autopsy

A man with a Scottish accent
calls to say he's found
a blank verse sonnet in her rib cage,
folded up like a love letter.
But I can hardly express
my disbelief before he moves on
to the haiku on the underside
of her eyelids, the pantoum
bracketed in vertebrae,
a rather bawdy limerick buried
in the saccharine junkyard
of her kidneys. *I didn't know,*
I say, as he lauds the ode
wreathing her navel, the erasure
where her thighs meet. He lowers
his voice, says he knows
we've asked to get her back
in ash-form, offers to read some
before feeding the rest to fire.
But this is where it ends,
thanks to the alarm clock
spurring me down the freeway
with the sun in my eyes.
So many exits before the real one.
Still, I can feel her beside me,
saying nothing, except to apologize
every time a bump causes
her arm to brush against mine.

State of the Union

All the news is talking
about the lack of surgical masks
and ice cream trucks for the dead,
how many grandfathers
need help to breathe,
but today, I can't seem to stop
wondering how oranges smell
when they're burning.
For that, too, is something
I've never known, having missed
my one chance to walk
a few blocks to a supermarket
that caught fire years ago,
the hoses too late, asparagus
like kindling, cans of pasta sauce
popping like firecrackers
they say, though men will say
anything to make up
for what they can't buy or steal:
wine bottles boiled dry,
rotisserie chickens charred
down to the size of a child's fist,
a forest of Bible-ply burnt
before it can even assist
those places we keep hidden,
and everywhere, puddles
of plastic flowing mercurially
between shelves that topple
whether you're looking or not.
But had I risen at the first sound,
the first engine's wail
lancing through my hangover,
I, too, might have stood so close
that every apolitical shift

in the night breeze taught me
something new about dairy aisles,
snap peas heat-forged
into arrowheads, and oranges:
what sweet mist they offer,
wept from the inside out.

If Couches Had Sphincters

That means, like us, they are born
with mouths that need feeding.

It doesn't matter that we can't see them.
How often have we pulled open

their guts to find the remote control
they mistook for mother's milk?

Sweet Christ, how they suffer:
all those shocks of spilled coffee,

chip crumbs like shards of glass,
toothy bouquets of house keys.

For us, they wreck their spines.
They sit naked in the dark, waiting.

And still we leave them on street corners
amidst all that dust and rain

without so much as an apology,
never mind how we'll feel later

as we sweep up the mess they used
every inch of their bodies to hide.

Connie Post

I try to construct my poems like unique architecture. I try to assure that the corridors ease into themselves. I hope to construct a space in the room that leaves the reader gazing. I strive to make doorways in and out of the poem that are both creative and accessible. As a poet, my goal is to use the most precise imagery that tells its own story. I enjoy making language and concepts interesting and unexpected. I try to use economy of language at every moment possible in the work. I want the reader to be surprised and intrigued and I want the poem to make them rethink long held ideas and or beliefs. This is why I try as often as possible to turn a phrase in my work. I try to enter my poem with no pre-determined agenda. I may have a few thoughts, or a single metaphor. I hold onto the images or lines that occur to me during the day. I place these on the foundation (the page) and see what I can build. I like it most when I surprise myself and I always hope the reader is surprised and leans into the poem with me. If one walks through a museum, one not only enjoys the artifacts themselves but the way they are hung, the way the rooms pick up the light, the way the sunlight reflects at different angles. In my poetry I strive to follow this same philosophy and place the words carefully in the museum hallways of poetry. I want the images to stay with the reader and I hope they want to return often to the language inside the verse. Finally, I aspire to make my endings power packed and toil to pull in all the elements of the poem to a crescendo of meaning. I hope to make the ordinary extraordinary and celebrate everything in between.

My Parent's House on the Market

It's been thirty years
since I traveled up this driveway

in the flower beds
I see the footprints
of an old criminal

I do not touch the front door
with the lewd and lascivious
handle

I don't touch anything

I stand at the entry way
and fall inside the empty rooms
left behind
like burnt forests

I remember
how the smoke
filled our rooms
how we ran, scurrying
like terrified animals
out of the trees
out of the house
to abusive marriages
and addictions that
whittled away our youth

I return today to the
cracked concrete
and smudged windows

and understand
how a tracker
will return years later
to retrieve
a small piece of clothing
from a dead tree

Visitation

I've stopped driving by the house
I've stopped even slowing down
when I go to that part of town

I can't stop
thinking about the new family
living there
taking baths
closing the blinds
turning down the beds

I want to go to the front door
and tell them the details
of every unsolved crime

I want to stand in the entry way
and tell them
about the years I was half alive
under the same roof
the years I couldn't
write my story
on the dingy walls
of the bathroom

I wonder if a house
can beg for mercy
when it is being haunted
by another's history

I wonder if the walls
understand
that the past and present
have no equator

I wonder if at times
just before they turn off
the lamp
they see a dark figure
lingering in the doorway

and for a moment
understand what it means
to drown in your own room

Postcard Placed in the Package I Sent to Mexico

I bought some tangerines
at the farmer's market today.
I'm sorry I can't send you more,
but postage just went up again
and all these letters
are getting lost in the mail

I wish you could have seen
how dark the figs were this year
the juice is still lingering
in the back house
of my sovereign mouth

I never told you
when I planted those trees
because I thought your hands
were too kind
for this earth

Walking Alone

I walk around my neighborhood
and spot a small dog alone
without an owner

I can tell he has not been bathed
for weeks
maybe longer

I try to catch his eye
but he is digging
for a half-buried bone
on a half dead lawn

I think I recognize
myself
somewhere in the dirt
somewhere in the grains
where the earthworms
carry my story

I stand at the edge
of the sidewalk
for a long while
and he finally he looks at me
as if he too
understands
that loneliness
is the coefficient of loss

Guidelines in a Pandemic

Don't touch anything
not the doorknob
nor elevator button
or the jagged space
between
your cleaved lungs

wear a mask
to protect others
wear a mask
to hide your cyanotic self
the blue of your lips
the exact hue
of the ocean
we've smothered

don't let the
dead whale's carcass
float too close
to your bed

the small bits of plastic
inside the remains
will remind you
of dying
with plastic in your body

as if they
were trying to tell
their own story

and the body bags
washing up to shore
were not our own

Driver's Side

I know the exact sound
of a garage door opening

the precise pitch
of an engine shutting off

you always ask me
how I know you are home
before you even open the door

later that night, I tell you about
the meticulous science of car sounds
how a young girl
knows when her father is home
hears the driver's side door
a thud to the sternum
even in sleep

she knows exactly
how many staggering
drunk steps
it him takes to get to the back door

she knows the smell
of exhaust and whiskey
and how they teach a girl
the alchemy of holding her breath

she knows
she will drive away some day
closing her own door
of the pale green 72 Chevy

no one in the passenger seat
nor the back
and the trunk full of college clothes
and eight tracks

the highway before her
and the long
resilient silence
of an open road

Kimberly Ann Priest

Simply put, I write to survive. Having been through a number of traumas and griefs in life, writing poetry facilitates processing those stories and clearing out my psyche while also allowing me to make shareable art. I love being creative. I love the good feeling that comes from investigating and ordering internal chaos into something linguistically and aesthetically attractive. In the words of an ancient poet, it is an exchange of *beauty for ashes*.

Having done so much personal work via narrative poetry (my preferred form), I have begun to recognize the value of using art to address internality—especially when that internality has been fragmented by traumatic life events. Sexual trauma is particularly disordering, and the more tools one can access to reframe this trauma, the less distressed the mind. At least, this is what I have found in my own poetic journey. I've been able to reduce symptoms of PTSD and feel more embodied with each narrative work-through.

My newest poems address PTSD, as well as the lives of women, including my own, with special attention to *migration, memory,* and *motherhood* due to dangerous or unexpected stressors. Personally, I have dealt with assault, domestic violence, and homelessness. While I realize that my circumstances are (sadly) not unique, I believe I've been unique in my willingness to publish these narratives. For women, there is often something to fear in their environments and a level of unease.

Which is why it was strange to write the poem "The World is Whatever We Choose to Make It," featured in this anthology. On one hand, as most women realize, each of us only have control over self and cannot really make the world "whatever" we choose. Danger exists and others' choices deeply impact our lived realities. But, on the other hand, intentional personal growth affects our environmental experience and can lead to a better experience in the world over time. Poetry helps me engage that growth and *making* of my world. In it and through it, I can create beauty, goodwill, healthy well-being, etc. to transform as much of my internal and external realities as possible.

Elegy for My Daughter Who Has Never Known a Paradise

Lake Michigan

She is dark coat and seed, blonde shock into the wind, the earth
rounding a bend of sand to greet her, lift a grassy spray,

splash up, always vanishing in her media feed by plastic or acid
or use of fossil fuels—the impending end to her not-yet

beginning. Yesterday, Atlantic; today, the Salish Sea.
What whale will consume her compassion? What plot of milkweed

will she harvest and weed? Even I attend the funeral of a stranger
in Mexico—his body discovered carved up among trees—

while my daughter spots Koalas burning in Australia,
asks me to hurry and see. We listen as a woman bursts from the bushes

shirtless, one singed mammal wrapped up in her tee, the phone
poised between our faces and the Great Lake before us,

cold waves pounding over its well-deserted beach. Should I tell her
this shoreline is also eroding, the sand dune sliding away

beneath her guileless feet? We have long known that zebra clams
are bothering these waters, but of *Brachionus Leydigii* and *Thermocyclops*

Crassus little is known. Ecologists say, they might harmlessly adapt
to the climate of Lake Erie—they also predict, they may not.

Spirit of the Animal

At an event dedicated to survivors of sexual assault
hosted by Central Michigan University

I have no sound for the hollow part
of my grief—my open mouth aggressively
windless, my body folded as a reed,
the force of a northerly breath too strong,
dividing my gut, cutting its current,
complicating the power of what feels so uncontainable
yet stays so contained. That long caw
of pain. Bay of wolf or hiss of cat—
the whole spirit of an animal invested in
its voice, the whole body pulling in
then pulling out, rising up, divorcing me
walking away, it being so
disappointed with my lack of posture—
the way the wolf or cat would at least
round their shoulders, form their face.
but I am too slain, too stunned
by what I did not see coming. Like the figure
on stage, mere stem of a woman explaining
the rape—not about the rape but *explaining* it
as though there is some reasonable shape
to irrational deeds; as though there is
a plot line, some *lesson learned*, she says.
She shuffles her feet, looks down at the floor,
a rag heap of bare whispers, wind whistling over
her lips; every woman thereafter admitting
she is wiser now than she was before—
this will not happen again, they say, shoulders
slumped, shuffled feet, eyes staring at
the floor, bodies swaying back and forth.

Upon Viewing Katrín Sigurdardóttir's 'Metamorphic'

at the Eli and Edythe Broad Art Museum, Michigan State University
/ craft paper / plaster / marble /

This tatty couch, that stiff chair, the calico floor strewn with a few somethings—
a child's room. All the gray relic of our worst imaginations set out spaciously
and patterned with blocks of soft sun pouring through gridded glass behind
and to the left—eye level. No bed. / *bland* / You could
walk right into the maze, sit down in the center, begin playing
/ *reconstructing* / but for the blurred bodies in the doorway watching. One shuffles
her feet, the other straightens her coat. Paid positions. How to explain
that, sometimes, we must get as close to a thing as we can, crawl into the faux
arrangement, lie on the couch, sit in the chair, pretend there is TV, drink
a glass of milk / *not there* / sitting on a little table. How to explain
the poems we write incessantly in the corner of the room, backed up against
/ *imaginary* / walls that keep us folded in place, the embrace of a few strewn
pillows, the / *unfurnished* / blanket we pull over shoulders
hunched against the backside of yet another chair, the toys, the thrown toys; you
there, me here—*he / she / they* reenacting memories, and the way there are not
pillows or blankets or diversions enough, nor contextualization / *hours of light* /.

At a Monastic Retreat in Erie, Pennsylvania

Pop of a water heater, crackle of beams, my
        small cabin sputtering,
the only machine in a landscape—
        one startled emotion into the next
calling the forest to attention,
        imaginations thriving in the otherwise
silence. Last night, I had to explain
        the wintering habits of nailed down
wood and how most things were not meant
        to be constrained in one place—
my daughter calling, afraid,
        as her father's house made similar sounds,
brilliant ghosts of cut pine fattening
        the noiseless night, and all her limbic
energy panicking. It's quiet here too,
        I say, *otherworldly* quiet—
desirable *and* unnerving. A large
        picture window voyeurs three sleek deer
against impressionist white, the landscape
        blossoming with snow this early Tuesday
morning as I hug a hot mug of coffee
        close to my chest, a distant stab
of sound swallowing their bodies in deep
        timber gray. *Do this*, I told my daughter
hunkered against her father's empty corner recliner:
        pull three tubes of paint
from your artist's satchel, add water and brushes,
        then canvas—now enter its blankness, wildly.

My Grandmother's Ashes

are somewhere, earth-born, and not ashes at all. Bone and sand
that scatter and remain. Particles
of time always filtering through, whetted, reshaped—always
excavatable. I kept the phone close and listened
to my cousin's voice as grandmother was dying, reading
Psalm 34—*we will not fear though the earth give way*, one
by one laying shell fragments I recently collected
from a shoreline atop the soil enclosing roots of plants growing
all over my apartment,
each thumb of new green that sprouts up, witness. *Though its waters
foam and roar*, she continues, stems and leaves reaching
for a bright spot of sun. *Though the mountains tremble
at its swelling*, my cousin drifts silent, her breath shallow as I sit
on the floor cradling a handful of shells,
rocking—in the future she will be mineral, calcium, phosphorus.

The World is Whatever We Choose to Make It

South Haven, Michigan

My daughter stares out at the horizon through a camera picturing
she and I in a midwestern landscape, flaming

pink blush of sunset against course cornstalks turned dark charcoal
for the eye to imagine the fields will never appear

any other way than the way she has seen them. *The world
is whatever we choose to make it,* she writes below the photograph

on Instagram, then turns the camera outward again,
this time to say *live however you want* and posts our elongated shadows

against the sidewalk in this small town where we spend a Saturday.
Yesterday, the trees were flocked with bronze and burnt orange hues,

but today they begin to shed their leaves and she asks us to *decide
what to do with the time that is given us.*

We round the corner of a street to see Lake Michigan—in her feed
she calls it *the ocean.* We both want to live

by the ocean someday. But, maybe, as she says,
we are already here: the shoreline, the breakers, the seashells we take.

Lindsey Royce

    I am obsessed with voice and sound in a poem, addicted to imagery that works perfectly to convey meaning while being interesting. Lately, I have been exploring more white-space in poems, that beautiful marriage of silence and the grace notes in between. What makes my poems recognizable as mine is that I don't copy anyone but take in elements I admire from other poets' work I love. In a good poem, I find strong feeling, glorious crafting, accessibility and surprise. Wanting to be let in to a poem, excessive irony and detachment leave me cold, although some distance in poems can fascinate me. A contradiction. In short, I sum up my aesthetic as my preference for bold, feeling, and well-crafted poems that take me into fascinating worlds of thought, emotion, and surprise.

If Only, Your Buttery Voice

If only I could summon you back to our bed,
    where abdomen to abdomen, and amid
our favorite plum cognac candles,
    we could make love one last time.
I want to hear your breath, a cello in my ear, stroke
    your sweaty back silky as lanolin, given
to me just one more time, and solid, real,
    not some LSD fantasy. I'd sacrifice my home
to bring you back. I'd never take
    for granted the panorama that was us.
And if rain jeweled our bedroom windows,
    then let it rain. Let me hold you again,
swallow every letter of your name, apologize
    for the ways I hurt you. Let me solve
the puzzle of where you are, bring you
    back to me for one more night. I promise
I won't fumble your gifts again, nor in anger,
    protest your heart never gave them.

Hawk-Like, I Circle

When he sleeps, I check his breathing.
Once, he would lie on his back, casually fling

an arm over his head. Sipping air,
afraid to inhale deep, now

he is fearful as the abused pup I freed.
My superhero Marine's gone feather light, sits

to dress and pee. His pant legs puddle around his ankles,
threaten to drown his waistband down.

While I pack my briefcase, he preps his feeding tube,
fills bags of medical gruel and water,

balances them on the IV tree: I see those bags,
false scales of justice, and cipher their bullshit: he's just 56.

As he secures the feeding line into his J-tube,
his bicep is wasted, skin crepe, his Shellback

tattoo with Neptune's face sags. All of him shrinks
like a sliver of soap in wet hands,

his physical fitness and prowess vanished, youth
swapped for wisdom forced on the dying.

He'll leave me. Where the hell is he going?
My strongman is full of zeal, unwilling to go.

He tells hospice nurses, *I won't sink with the ship,
don't count me out, I'm hoping for a miracle*—

But in secret, he tells me, *I guess I'm dying,*
and eyes locked, I can't look away, or offer hope or disagree.

Walking Point

John scolded me unless I wore a wool jacket
and practical leather hiking boots
outdoors.

      He didn't like "city girl"

stilettos in bed because shoes just dirtied
the sheets.

~

      For romance, fishing
and hiking were his sensuality.

~

Early on, I bought in. John walked point, breaking
brush

for me, our fishing rods held safely high
to get to prime holes.

But too often, he lost grip of a branch,
      and it slapped my eye or cheek, and I'd yowl.

Impatient that I wasn't as tough as a recruit,
He might call me *baby* or *soft*.

~

We took marathon hikes along rivers that slithered
like ribbons strewn on Christmas carpets.

~

John taught me how to fly cast, where to throw
the line, how to strip it to tease
                                the big fish
away from banks where they hid, to *piss them off*

        so they'd strike.

~

He helped me reel in plenty of 20-plus inchers,
but guilty about stressing the trout, twisting

out hooks, and scared to hold their slimy, wriggling
for the photo,

I asked to fish less often, so we hunted
mushrooms instead.

~

                Never taking the easy path,

John bushwhacked to reach secret spots
where we found morrells, chanterelles, and oysters

to cook or sell to his chef buddies.

~

John walked point,

as he'd done in the infantry, taking the most exposed
position, putting his body between mine
and predators— bears, moose, mountain lions—
   and commanding his Akbash, Callie, to rear-guard.

~

And if I fell over a log or slipped in the river,
filling my waders like fatal balloons,

John dropped his rod and sloshed over to help me,
as that man, friend and love,
       couldn't bear to see me hurt.

Bacon-Wrapped Dates
And The Last Word

Stones pock our dirt road to the end of my vision.
                There, perspective hones to a point
as small as your vaccine scar.   You were making
        bacon-wrapped dates for a Thanksgiving party,

and I recall wishbones, that like all superstitions,
are archived with chuckles from past holidays
        where you sliced turkey so gently, the meat
could have been butter.

   What sacrifice
        is in the filigree of a dead geranium's blush, one
inhabiting that soon-forgotten hovering
between life and death, the last inhale,   the letting go,
        the book's last word,   cinema's fade-to-black?

I forget what breakfast juice I sipped while you stiffened,
your gregarious green eyes waiting to be plucked.

This year, I'll try to cook Thanksgiving potluck,
use spices you left behind, your oregano, your sage,
no mary jane to lose this holiday wholly to fantasy,
        this grave anniversary of the beginning of your end.

There is nothing uniform about grief,
though I'd scissor it into islands
like the Cyclades,   their trees, pomegranate and fig,
        fruit sweet after the bacon-wrapped dates

you'd been cooking before you collapsed,
and the ambulance squared up the drive.
Your food was left warm on the counter.
                      How could I have known you'd begun
to leave this life while you were making side dishes?

Who could have suspected your cranberry tart
would foreshadow the color of the body bag
    zipped slowly over   your perfect face.

The Fuck-You Facelift

The friend with the leopard-spotted neck tattoo
tumbling down her shoulder cattle-prods me

to big up my breasts, to remove the double chin
that hangs, scroll-like, threatening to unroll.

I point out my figure flaws, that geometry of lines
batiked around my mouth, and John says, of the chin,

Lose weight; it ain't cancer. I counter with,
I want to see a fancy doctor, get what's dumpling-like

fixed, quick as it would take to drench
in a hot bath. On the surgical table I'd lie, eyes

wrinkled as wicker, bags the doc would sculpt
as smooth as a cello. He never denies

I'm attractive, but he doesn't call me
pretty or *hot*. Instead, he argues against vain

procedures, like laser-toasting my décolletage
or my desire to get what sags lifted, as if my face

could defy gravity. *You'll look like a waxed fruit.*
He says, *Why not get a tummy tuck, too,*

so you can have a pubic beard? I want to be pretty
and thin as a spider lily with boobs.

Don't get those done, he says, *They'll feel funny.*
I finish my dessert, rise from the table,

overgrown as ever, and I wait in the hush
to hear, *You're beautiful as you are.*

When he's silent, I decide that when he dies, I'll
take the life insurance to the plastic surgeon.

I'll be so beautiful, so ridiculously irresistible—
he'll come back home to me, just to see.

First Christmas Without You

I pass the grapes and loaf to no one,
set the teapot between two cups.

I tear the heel off your sourdough, dip
it into your homemade oil, luminous

gold-green pool on a white plate.
A yeast of sorrow bloats in my throat,

as Christmas carols shatter the silence.
My red sweater, your twinkling lights,

the reflection of colors on the curve of a glass.
I never understood how much I needed you to sustain me.

Under the blanket, we lay dying.
At the time, I thought it was only you.

Barbara Ungar

My most recent chapbook, *EDGE*, takes its name from the Evolutionarily Distinct and Globally Endangered species lists. While my first book, *Thrift*, included a poem on global warming, my earlier work was primarily concerned with life in a woman's body, to paraphrase Virginia Woolf, always seen refracted through myth and science, connecting to larger forces: the personal as political. My most recent full-length collection, *Save Our Ship*, is a cry for attention to our precarious position, "sawing off the limb on which we are perched," as Paul Ehrlich puts it, in one of the epigraphs to *EDGE*.

In *EDGE*, I focus specifically on a dozen or so of the countless species now endangered by our own. Expanding that chapbook into a full-length volume, rather than writing about more endangered species, I find my work has turned toward how to go on balancing on the razor's edge: how to stay alert and try to wake others up, to fight and not despair. As I experience my own aging alongside the maturing of my son, I seem to find balance by, on the one hand, confronting and accepting my personal mortality, while on the other, attempting to confront (if not accept) the possibility of species mortality, including that of our own. How to live in the Anthropocene, how to bear witness to the sixth extinction, without giving up? For me, the best answer seems to be to look at the biggest picture possible: to consider the birth and death of the universe, and of every galaxy, star, and planet within it, to put our losses into perspective. "One Art." At the same time, I marvel at the most minute wonders of creation, and know that they will continue, whether or not we are here to write and read poems about them.

Star Apple

any way you slice it
inside each apple a star
around seeds black as holes

from which a tree might
root branch leaf and bloom
as at the center of each galaxy a black hole

unknowable as our growing universe
mostly dark matter & energy
inexplicable as any apple

could you build one
no though you might pick or paint one
matter and energy inextricably

knotted in the fruit
that fell for Newton
as for Eve

Kabbalah's tree of life blows
from a spark
of impenetrable darkness

any way you slice it
stars fall from apples
holes seed our sky

the tongue loves the apple
as the night sky loves the star

Resolutions for 2021

1. Stop worrying
2. Embrace death with your whole heart, as Lao Tsu instructs
3. Ski up Potash Mountain
4. Name the stars
5. Converse with the dead
6. Give birth while hibernating
7. Write a book in classical Japanese
8. Swim across the lake underwater
9. Take a train around the world
10. Pick up every piece of plastic
11. Learn the language of animals
12. Practice daily levitation
13. Say goodbye to everything
14. Canoe from Manhattan to Canada
15. Remember all your dreams
16. Discover a new butterfly
17. Become carbon neutral
18. Grow your own fur
19. Forgive yourself and everyone else
20. Taste like a peach
21. Sweep the footprints off the moon

Stone Soup

Who, if his son asks for bread, would give him
a stone? Maybe the father of the fairy shrimp:
three hundred species, from Antarctica
to deserts to frozen mountain lakes.
Some have no dads—parthenogenesis.
All can go dormant: in diapause, as cysts,
they can withstand drought, frost, desiccation,
radiation, salt, even the vacuum of space,
for centuries—then, carried by currents
or predators or winds, stirred back to life
by the ephemeral waters of spring pools
all over the Midwest, they cruise, supping
on algae soup, feeding mallards and fish.
Who needs any more miracle than this?

Quadruple Virgo

I don't worry about the universe expanding
      an inhalation of dark matter
            the Secret One slowly growing a body

or our galaxy
      a white cat stretched
            across black sheets

I don't worry about the solar system
      though our sun will burn out like any furnace

or our planet that can scrape us off like mold
      wash away our trash
            and mix up some new concoctions

I do worry about our paranoid-
      schizophrenic States

I don't worry about upstate so far
      from fire & floods
           so far

I worry they're killing the horse
      that laid the golden Saratoga

I don't worry about my little house
      needs some work but
           has stood across three centuries

I worry about taxes computers
      & succumbing to plague
           or eventual dementia

I don't worry about the streams of microscopic life
        flowing in warm currents up my legs & trunk
                into my nose

or about my cells
        despite the spiked invader
                the bats' revenge

I never worry about my ten octillion atoms
        my quarks and leptons
                doing their quantum Lindy

I don't worry about the mostly empty space
        inside & out

just that infinitesimal crosshair of infinity
        where the loops of the sideways-eight meet
                between macro and micro

my particular X-marks-the-spot
        or black dot
                on my lottery ticket

Lonesomest George

(ACHATINELLA APEXFULVA)

How to sing the loneliness of George,
last of his kind, bred and dead in a lab
in Hawaii, extinction capital of the world?

A hermit who rarely emerged from his shell.

What for? No forest,
no one to mate with,
till he died of old age.
14 years in solitary.

People used to walk up the hill
shaking trees, collecting bucketsful
clustered thick as berries.

In the 30s, Japanese brought in
giant African land snails as pets:
a foot long, they ate everything.

In the 50s, the rosy wolfsnail
brought from Florida to eat the giant snails
preferred the 750 native kinds instead.

Hawaii was the most magical place on Earth
with beautiful, rainbow-colored snails hanging from the trees,
said Melissa, molecular ecologist.
This entire group is about to fall
off the face of the planet.

We've all broken down and cried in the field,
said David, the last to see 20 kinds in the wild.
He started the love shack,
a captive breeding program in a trailer
where George ended his days
alone in his terrarium
among 2,000 other snails on the brink.
Hermaphroditic, some snails can reproduce
solo, but not George.

Named for Lonesome George,
the last Pinta Island tortoise.

In native legend tree snails are revered
as the voice of the forest.

No one now can remember how to hear them.

Dream Of Myself

looking in a mirror
swathed in black lace

human shape translucent
and pulsing like a jelly-

fish heart and womb
shining through like the Visible

Woman's wondrous as
the Piglet octopus

with its crown of tentacles
and saucer eyes or

the pocket shark shaped
like a palm-sized sperm whale

the caterpillar fringed
like a Mardi Gras float

or Uncle Walt marveling
at how his ankles bend

Never worry about beauty again
You too are God in drag

Alexandrine Vo

I grew up in war-torn Vietnam, under conditions of extreme poverty and hardship. I was born after my father returned home from serving seven years in Communist concentration camps in Dong Nai Province, Vietnam, after which he continued to serve three more years under house arrest.

As the youngest child of this South Vietnamese Army officer and prisoner, I witnessed up-close the punishing vestiges of war that my father carried, which remained perfectly intact throughout the years thereafter, leaving deep impressions upon our family. This is the place I write from, to call out the memories I have stored in my body that have been so weighty and persistent, to capture that world in the most visceral ways possible, exorcising in words the distillation of my dreams and imagination via the rite of passage of time.

Each of my poems coalesced quickly. However, I have often re-written and painstakingly edited, spreading my work over the period of ten years. Many of these poems from my first manuscript are about violence, hunger, desperation, loss, bewilderment, the wish for non-division, and the havoc political structures can impress upon ordinary human lives. They are songs that marry peaceful pastoral scenes with some of the most lightless moments.

One day I left my home and woke up in another county as an exile. Nevertheless, these poems caught up and squeezed themselves through the years, writing themselves out of me. Every step of the way, I felt life funneling me towards poetry and what I urgently needed to lay down onto the page. I am deeply humbled that my parents' sufferings have allotted me the inheritances of a second language and country, which have opened the doors for these poems to come tumbling through.

OMPHALOS

in the middle of the body is a door   that opens one way

locks behind you   with a cold

precision   suddenly you are there   gazing at eternity

with your timorous eyes of an injured bird   since the way

back is lost   the tether cut   the vessel hollow—

how?   far from home   you seize the first mantle of flesh

trust sinews and bones   the shock of air contra blood

and viscera   the hovering in that nothing-wanting dark

so cold the water now   but it is *may*   may

your father pacing smoking   your sister home to put the pot on

your mother who has this one reason to laugh   on emerald thighs

of mountain   where bees gather   to brew your name

Souffle au Cœur

I.

Always it begins in the kitchen. Kerosene wets
the wick and silhouettes trot across the room.

The black dog waits beneath the table
for a windfall, a fish skeleton or egg shell.

Outside, crickets murmur. A waft of night wind
between loments of chrysophylla.

Hens roost atop the pig pen,
thronging in a mass of brown plume.

A hammock lies slackened, expectant
of the weight it must contain.

Bamboo rods stack neatly in one corner,
stiff fibers flaring on their bulk.

In a windowless room,
your hands wring us. Fingers, nails, and palms.

II.

Like an island on the table, lonely with its wick
extinguished,

its oil, cold within the orb of its body, wherefrom the world
is a glassy, viridian film.

Disintegration answers. We wake to wreckage,
to broken things.

The hens and their beady eyes.
Painted pine moth caterpillars masticating leaves.

A black tarantula
cascading across the yard from its broad net.

Nothing and no one notices
the things that come undone. All around us

is every sign of spring.
Even the swallows are laughing in the ruffles of pine skirts.

III.

We were digging into grandmother's betel leaves   and areca nuts, looking for white lime,   a wet jar of caustic mush for tattooing the teeth.   A walking-stick creature

needed to get to heaven.   Just one swab and he was good to go. But where is it.   The pesky quails have been meddling again,   breaking up earth,   mining

chrysanthemum roots.   I can see their tracks, remnants of worms: signs of work in piecemeal.   They retreat back into the dark   where we cannot catch them.

Last night at dinner,   we were silent all evening. We were waiting for father   and what he was planning to do.   Bodies filing into the room,   we plumped down with stoic faces.   Between dire shadows cast

on chairs.   Spoons beside bowls towing their own

shade.   Our father brings a hammer to the dinner table.

IV.

Impossible to know what secrets the wind
tells the night, for whom
it gestures in such damp darkness.

Only sighing leaves, boughs and roots.
They share with the birds
all that we don't know.

We heed these bones,
these late folios,
against a page of vague and starless sky.

Through the eaves,
wind shivers and stirs. Dogs counter barks
with barks and looped baying.

Here in this sphere
of salt and stone:
only the night, whatever night has known.

V.

Awake and quiet
as sea swallows circle and cry.

By morning only the fowls and
lowing cows remain.

For years
I have been waiting.

Now in a rush words come.
In modest attires

in black coats of eveningwear.
As if something

in the hems of space and lines
frees.

As though soothing
all my sleeping ancient terrors.

Vestments

I.

How will things grow in a season like this?

Sun turned skin to fractured nets,
cracked and ashen to the touch.

The shoulders darkening,
then the forearms, two twigs
I used for fanning.

To eat was hard, much less
to sleep, to breathe!
Forgive my lips their small divorce.

Such summers that we could not bear.

II.

And yet my father, with pulpy loam between his toes,
        heaved vessels of water from the stream.

        River to paddy, river to paddy, such mindless repetition
        that even the vessels sunk
into senselessness, tired
        of hoisting, sagging down as a sow's low belly. The water
          waking the tender field to parched murmurs.

At day's end, he collapses on the bend,
        heart pounding through ribcage, breath cast down
          like ripe peach falling.

III.

To his wedding, my father wore a grey suit, bespoke and paid
                      with borrowed money.

                    Not knowing what to name his children
he cast the die among flowers and incense,
                      loving that smell of heady resin.

      Studious, he was not born to bear arms,
preferring books to shells, late afternoons
                        on the sun-warmed darkness of a water buffalo's back.

                A devout man, anxious about heaven,
        he spends late life atoning.

IV.

He will not speak much of the dead. Not speak
of pain or hunger, war or torture, how many and where.

Merely lets the silence consume
our small beleaguered home.

Father, the killer, the victim: a dead man
living, haunted and pursued.

Ghosts stalk through his dreams and he wakes
to cold paralysis. His days are hemmed in
by the innumerable voices

arguing among themselves.

Revisiting

Little city my city   in rustic splendor
under terracotta eaves   a wing-boned roof

With your four totems
a bed of planks on which we have slept

How cool beneath us   aging in the night
this wood's stern air

      Even the drowse of soot is home
         even the thrum of pig bristles

lulls   rustling in the dark   while the dirt floor
primps and waits

Fifteen years in exile   still every room harbors
a lingering scent of war

This house that   empty   grieves like a widow
Ribs and skulls sleep soundly in the soil

Jeanne Wagner

When I read over the titles of the poems featured here in the *Aeolian Harp Anthology*, I saw Dr. Frankenstein discussing love, Charon the boatman being interviewed on Jimmy Kimmel, my mother compared to bees. I admit, when choosing a subject for a poem, or rather when a subject chooses me, I seem to go straight for the incongruous: the odd pairings, the mythical resurrected in the contemporary, religious parallels cropping up unexpectedly in the secular. I see poetry, and all creative writing, as a way to discover, through the instrument of words, our hidden selves, with all their loves and obsessions. I want a poem to run away with me as I'm writing it, so that I'm simultaneously author and passenger. I usually begin with a small fixation or recurrent memory, then follow where the words are taking me. I try to write lyrical, imagistic poetry that avoids the predictable and that has a certain otherworldliness. Over the years I've only written a few poems that live up to my own expectations. Some of them appear in this anthology. I hope you will like them too.

Backyard Birds

Bird

More song than body
more flight than time
it doesn't fit in itself
or in all its days

—Ulalume González de León

I have these recurrent dreams

where I find tiny vulnerable creatures

nesting in my closet.

I've spent a lifetime neglecting them,

then suddenly, there they are,

wasting away in some corner of my sleep,

wide-eyed and forgotten.

For years I'd wake up and find myself crying

for some motherless litter,

though lately it's been feathery things,

badly fledged.

Once, to my shock, it was a baby with an old face

I'd birthed without even noticing, all falling

off the grid of my life

like those backyard birds whose names I never knew,

or briefly learned, and now they're vanishing

by the millions,

gone before I can recognize a single one

by its feathers or beak.

It's hard to love something that keeps on leaving,

whose name slips away from the tongue,

whose song dissolves in the air

like breath.

I remember how my mother, who never

tended much to growing things,

showed us a robin's nest in a coiled-up clothesline

that hung from a hook in the yard.

She pulled up a ladder so we could peer in,

but not touch,

their shells possessive and beautiful,

their fetal hearts specks of invisible thrum,

she said would be their souls,

if they had souls.

No can one tell me how to fit into a self,

though I still rescue the odd window-bashed bird

made docile by shock,

or the cat's trophy catch, its heart haranguing

its chest, and for a few seconds

I'll hold it inside my palm,

its body more body than flight

Doctor Frankenstein on Love

I gave him everything I love.
The high forehead,
which looks so endearing on babies,
on his face
became a frightening cliff-drop
of skull,
and the vacant eyes,
with their hint of lethal hurt,
were the same cornflower-blue irises
I plucked
from the beggared sockets
of the dead.

I thought we could live again,
like memory,
that we would rise from unrequited
flesh
as only bodies carefully stitched
from remnants can.

But he lurches like an old film
unspooling
and dreams in a language
not his own.
Sometimes just the white amnesia
of a flower
makes him weep.

Charon Talks to Jimmy Kimmel

It's a job, somewhere between docent and
    designated driver.

I wear the drag of the underworld dead,
    but I dream a lot.

There's never any hurry, never any weather.
    The sky a pall.

What can the wind say that hasn't already
    been said?

I prefer peaceful: no sound of an outboard
    splitting the air, no discord,

no pull cord lashing the engine to life. Just
    the flat swoosh of an oar.

Bottom line, it's an easy task: no time clocks,
    no quotas to ignore.

I could practice the chthonic arts in my sleep.
    Often do.

I play disheveled, with carious teeth and stub
    of a stogie, breath of

over-heated coffee. What's more like hell
    than that singed odor,

oily and dark as this river at night? Sometimes
    I can smell their fear.

That's when I sing to them, shades – if you'll
    pardon the pun –

of Venetian gondolier or Volga Boatmen.
    It's all about atmosphere.

But no dirges, no keening, no lullabies. Even
    the young are old here,

everyone on the lookout for metaphor. Passing
    is like that, the senses keener.

They notice how pliable sound is at night, how fog
    rises to form

a wreath in the air. The way light bends in the water,
    like a broken bone.

My Mother Was Like the Bees

because she needed a lavish taste
on her tongue,
a daily tipple of amber and gold
to waft her into the sky,
a soluble heat trickling down her throat.
Who could blame her
for starting out each morning
with a swig of something furious
in her belly, for days
when she dressed in flashy lamé
leggings like a starlet,
for wriggling and dancing a little madly,
her crazy reels and her rumbas,
for coming home wobbly
with a flicker of clover's inflorescence
still clinging to her clothes,
enough to light the darkness
of a pitch-black hive.

Dogs That Look Like Wolves

When my dog hears the neighbor's baby cry, he begins
to howl, his head thrown back. He's all heartbreak and
hollow throat, tenderness rising in each ululation. He's
a saxophone of sadness, a shepherd calling for his stray.
I've read that baying is both a sign of territory and
a reaching out for whatever lies beyond: home and loss,
how can they be understood without each other?
Once I had an outdoor dog who sang every day at noon
when the Angelus belled from the corner church.
She was a plain dog, but I could prove, contrary to all
the theologians, that at least once a day she had a soul.
I've always loved dogs that look like wolves, loved
stories of wolves: the alphas, the bullies, the bachelors.
We have to forgive them when they break into our
fenced-off pastures, lured by the lull of a grazing herd,
or a complacent flock, heads bent down. Prey, it's called.
At night wolves chorus into the trackless air, the range
of their song riding far from their bodies till they think
the stars will hear it and be moved, almost to breaking,
while my poor dog stands alone on the deck, howling
into the canyon's breadth, as if he's like me, looking
for a place where his song will carry. Dogs know,
if there is solace to be had, their voice will find it.
This air is made for lamentation.

In My Dreams It's Autumn

Scarlet bleeding through the veins of leaves

with no one to stanch the flow,

and me looking for a fixative, saline,

or that old standby formalin,

to keep my dreams from weeping shape and color,

to stop my inner landscapes from deforming

like a Dali watch face,

old lovers from shapeshifting into strangers,

and the dead, with their shy, disembodied smiles,

from slipping away again.

Why do the lost return if we can't hold them,

can't make their sweet resurrections take

root, if only for a night?

Like the ghost with my grandmother's voice,

her skin soft as a worn blanket?

Why can't she rest awhile before, *whoosh*, she's gone

and the streets begin their unraveling?

I keep a dream atlas in my head,

a small town of unrequited avenues,

the trees just beginning to blaze.

Leaves the color of flames.

Martin Willitts Jr.

I am curious and constantly excited by the world. I want to know more about what is happening in the world, and become a reporter for the news of what I have seen, heard, or experienced. I am an old-fashioned oral storyteller, telling myths, legends, and folk tale stories from memory, and sometimes this method appears in my poems like "Calligraphy Brush" which I created. Or I will take a belief like how the dead can haunt various objects (like in Japan) and re-tell the belief in "Ghosts."

I am also interested in form, especially the pure villanelle, in which the pattern exactly repeats, word for word, the first and third lines. It is like a high wire act. And, I dared to write a poem based on my favorite poet, Jane Kenyon. I know it is something special when it has been in archives twice. As a child, I played classical music in a local orchestra, so I am familiar with the constraints of form.

Some poems seem to arrive from a strange place like "The Suggestion of Birds." I thought the poem was going to go in one direction but it went somewhere else. I decided to let the poem tell me what it wanted to say. I also used to be a Jazz musician, so I am used to improvisation. The poem was basically an invented story.

"A Leading" is one of those poems that did not want to end. I decided to link sections with the last line to the next section's first line. I don't know where this form evolved or if I created it, but I did this once before, years ago, and I always wanted to try it again. In many ways, it is a form as much as repeating the first and third lines in villanelles. It also works as a call-and-response in music. Each end and beginning become an echo. In music, this would be called a sustained note. In each case, the mood and theme changes meaning and focus.

Bone-Chilled

These mountains were not high enough to have snowcaps,
but a toddler tugged on his mother's sleeve
as a silent plea for safety. The pond was frozen over,
although spring was coming out of its cabin,
carrying a berry-picking tin pail. The boy shivered
in his parka, back-glancing at the junipers
where the all-day bird was singing, knowing weather
was purposely fickle. His mother had pushed off
the latest attempt by another no-account guy
who had stared once too intently at his eight
year old sister. Bone-chills emanated from that man,
like a kind of mean wind blasting them in the face.

He went with his mother, searching with a group
for his sister who had run off into this direction,
into the folds of the mountains. The boy called out
in his small voice, loudly for the lost,
already dreading what he knew must be true and too late.
His mother, biting at her cold sore, seemed serene
at this same awful conclusion, holding one boot
belonging to his sister, strangely smaller,
like hope, like one blue flower in the snow-melt.

Calligraphy Brush

It is said first woman sang cherry blossoms
until a horse emerged out of the mists. It is said
she took hairs from its tail, which went here
to there, further than a dragon's fire, further
than blossoms float in strong wind as tiny fans.
It is said she used the hairs to make the first brush,
like whispers of her eyelashes, softer than mist.
She drew a horse chasing freedom, its tail on fire,
spreading the scent of blossoms there to here.
It is said that first word was made this way,
each word falling scales from a shedding dragon.
It is said this is how stars were made from ink.
Who said these things? Sone say lies floated petals,
here and there, swishing truth at mayflies.

Dip your brush into plum blossom ink,
make the mark with the word for woman
onto rice paper from the forbidden garden.
Your words mist, gallop out of paper,
flapping dragon wings delicate as a woman's lashes.

Lies float there to here, near paper lanterns, as moths.

Ghosts

In feudal Japan, they believed ghosts lived
in stick-like wands. Angry ghosts
stamped their feet like children wanting their way
for what was bad for them.

Ghosts visited as unwanted guests
refusing to leave, not even when shown the way
to the nearest exit. Maybe, the ghosts needed hats
of thatched straw to ward off rain.

Many problems come with ghosts.
Do they need a rice bowl; or is that too much?
Why do they sweep moonlight off the floors?
They never walk without tripping on floor cracks.

They never have eyes.
But, when you see them
do not assume they are blind.
They hear concern.

Let Death Come

Villanelle, starting with a line from Jane Kenyon

Let evening come — I am not afraid of dying
for I have known the kindness of birds and seed.
Let trouble find someone else. I have time

to find the climbing blue flowers, trying
to talk to God. Let winds tear, let rivers recede,
let evening come — I am not afraid of dying.

None of this will succeed in denying
what I know is true: not one will impede.
Let trouble find someone else, I have time

before I die, to search for God, and find
bees hording secrets and worms for bird feed—
let evening come, I am not afraid of dying

in the winter of my life, in everlasting, crying,
searching. Death will have me, even if I plead:
Let trouble find someone else. I have time,

I have time; I can fit more love in my mind
and heart. Let the turtles try to hide in reeds,
let evening come — I am not afraid of dying.
Let trouble find someone else — I have time.

The Suggestion of Birds

Where the man walked, the earth broke away
into distant futures, a deluge of sadness.
The earth broke like a stick at the suggestion of birds.
It sounded like knitting needles making a sweater
from skeins knowing intense panic.
He had seen a red-winged blackbird
for the first time, and it moved as bedroom curtains
when two people make love behind them.

It is crucial to have such moments: to see
the unexpected when no one else is looking.
He did not have to share this with just anyone.
He could hoard it. His hungry eyes were filled with it.

When he walked, the earth broke into music
from a field of red poppies.
Never mind the harvesters reaping them for drugs,
or the music escaping like bees.
Never mind the translators of the unknown. Never mind
his blue sweater perfect for hiking into the lemon remoteness.

A blackbird with a red patch on its wing studied the man
with equal curiosity. It was deciding if it should sing.

A Leading

In blue irises, in the remnant of wind,
in the fox prints of clouds in the night sky
making no sounds, somewhere
where you want to be, you are in a covenant
with light. Light rains,
calling your name. I give you this
in a laughing steadiness.
Almost perfect responses are being transplanted.
In this room beginning to rim with blue shadows
from blinding sunlight, you are rendered with love.

PUBLICATION CREDITS

Scott Ferry

"Wasting"—*Abbey*

"Box" — *Madness Muse*

"Don / Doff" — *Misfit*

"unbody" — *Gleam: Journal of the Cadralor*

"Eviction" — *Rye Whiskey Review*

"Streetlights" *Cathexis Press Northwest*

"After I Find my Daughter's Betta Dead" — *New York Quarterly*

Kari Gunter-Seymour

"I Come From a Place So Deep Inside America It Can't Be Seen" — *Anthology of Appalachian Writers, Volume XII*, 2020

"Hooper Ridge Girl" — *Rascal 2019*

"I Spoke To You of Stars Instead" — *From A Place So Deep Inside America It Can't Be Seen* (Sheila-Na-Gig Editions 2020)

"Bethal Ridge Cemetery" — *Stirring: A Literary Collection*, Winter 2020

"Hold Fast" — *Still: The Journal*, Fall 2020

Michael Meyerhofer

"For Ahmaud Arbery…" — *Rattle*, May 9, 2020.

"Urban Legend" — *Orchard Review. Vol. 23, No. 2.*, October, 2018.

"A Belated Apology…" — *National Poetry Review* (November, 2018) and *Verse Daily* (Dec. 24, 2018).

"My Mother's Autopsy" — *River Styx.* Issue 103/104. 2020.

"State of the Union" — *MAYDAY Magazine.* January 18, 2021.

"If Couches Had Sphincters" — *FRiGG.* Fall/Winter, 2020.

Connie Post

"Postcard Placed in the Package I Sent to Mexico" — *Up the Staircase Quarterly*

"Guidelines in a Pandemic" — *Califragile*

Kimberly Priest

"Elegy for My Daughter Who Has Never Known a Paradise" — *Salamander*

"Spirit of the Animal" — *Borderlands*

"Upon Viewing Katrín Sigurdardóttir's 'Metamorphic'" — *The Harbor Review*

"The World is Whatever We Choose to Make It" — *About Place Journal*

Barbara Ungar

"Lonesomest George" — *EDGE* (Ethel Press 2020)

"Dream of Myself" — *Pedestal* (2019).

Alexandrine Vo

"Omphalos," — *Two Countries Anthology: U.S. Daughters and Sons of Immigrant Parents*

"Souffle au Couer," — *Salamander*

"Vestments," — *The Stinging Fly*

"Revisiting," — *The Stinging Fly, Two Countries Anthology: U.S. Daughters and Sons of Immigrant Parents*

Jeanne Wagner

"Backyard Birds" — *Nimrod International Journal*

"Dr. Frankenstein on Love" — *RHINO*

"Charon Talks to Jimmy Kimmel" — *Spillway*

"Dogs That Look Like Wolves" — *Nimrod International Journal*

"My mother was like the bees" — *California Quarterly*

Martin Willitts Jr.

"Bone-Chilled" — Autumn Sky Poetry Daily

"Calligraphy Brush" — *Comstock Review*, reprinted in the anthology *Silk & Spice*, (Glass Lyre Press, 2016) and was nominated for the 2016 Liakoura Prize.

"Ghosts" — *Silk & Spice* (Glass Lyre Press, 2016)

"Let Death Come" — *Autumn Sky Poetry Daily* and appeared in *Autumn Sky Poetry Daily Archives*, 2017 and 2021.

"The Suggestion of Birds" — *Nine Mile Magazine*

"A Leading" — *Paterson Review*

Contributor Notes

Scott Ferry helps our Veterans heal as a RN. In other lives he taught high school, practiced acupuncture, and managed aquatic centers. He has recent work in *American Journal of Poetry, Cultural Weekly, Spillway, Misfit*, among others. He has two books of poetry: *The only thing that makes sense is to grow* (Moon Tide, 2020) and *Mr. Rogers kills fruit flies* (Main St. Rag, 2020). His third chapbook, *Sea of Marrow*, is upcoming from Ethel in early 2022. He lives in the great Pacific Northwest and loves to garden, swim, and make his family laugh.

Kari Gunter-Seymour's poetry collections include *A Place So Deep Inside America It Can't Be Seen* (Sheila-Na-Gig Editions 2020) winner of the 2020 Ohio Poet of the Year Award; and *Serving* (Crisis Chronicles Press 2018/2020) runner up, Yellow Chair Review Chapbook Contest. Her poems appear in numerous journals and publications including *Verse Daily, Rattle, The NY Times*, and on her website: www.kariguntersermourpoet.com. Her work was selected by former US Poet Laureate Natasha Trethewey to be included in the PBS American Portrait crowdsourced poem, *Remix: For My People* and a poem she wrote in support of families living in poverty in Athens County, OH, went viral and was seen by over 100,000 people, resulting in thousands of dollars donated to her local food pantry. Gunter-Seymour has provided poetry workshops to incarcerated teens and adults and women in recovery as well as teaching an ongoing series of monthly generative workshops. She hosts a seasonal performance series "Spoken & Heard," featuring poets, writers and musicians from across the country. A ninth generation Appalachian, she is the founder/executive director of the Women of Appalachia Project (WOAP) (www.womenofappalachia.com) and editor of the WOAP anthology series, *Women Speak*, volumes 1-6. She is the Poet Laureate of Ohio.

Michael Meyerhofer's fifth book of poetry, *Ragged Eden*, was published by Glass Lyre Press. His other books are *What To Do If You're Buried Alive* (Split Lip Press), *Damnatio Memoriae* (winner of the Brick Road Poetry Book Contest), *Blue Collar Eulogies* (Steel Toe Books, finalist for the Grub Street Book Prize), and *Leaving Iowa* (winner of the Liam Rector First Book Award). He has also published five chapbooks: *Pure Elysium* (winner of the Palettes and Quills Chapbook Contest), *The Clay-Shaper's Husband* (winner of the Codhill Press Chapbook Award), *Real Courage* (winner of the Terminus Magazine and Jeanne Duval Editions Poetry Chapbook Prize), *The Right Madness of Beggars* (winner of the Uccelli Press 3rd Annual Chapbook Competition), and *Cardboard Urn* (winner of the Copperdome Chapbook Contest). Individual poems won the Marjorie J. Wilson Best Poem Contest, the Laureate Prize for Poetry, the James Wright Poetry Award, and the Annie Finch Prize for Poetry. He is the Poetry Editor of *Atticus Review* and also the author of a fantasy series. For more information and an embarrassing childhood photo, please visit www.troublewithhammers.com.

Connie Post served as the first Poet Laureate of Livermore, California from 2005 - 2009. Her work has appeared in *Calyx, Comstock Review, Blue Fifth Review, I-70 Review, One, River Styx, Dogwood, Slipstream, Spoon River Poetry Review, Valparaiso Poetry Review, The Slippery Elm, Spillway, The Pedestal Magazine,* and *Verse Daily*. Connie's awards include the Crab Creek Review Award, the Caesarea Award, the Liakoura Award, the Dirty Napkin Cover Prize, and first prize in the Prick of Spindle annual competition. Her work has appeared in several anthologies including *Alongside we Travel, Contemporary Poets on Autism* (NYQ books), *A Bird as Black as the Sun, Truth to Power: Writers Respond To The Rhetoric Of Hate And Fear* (Cutthroat: A Journal of the Arts, 2017), *Carrying the Branch* and *Collateral Damage* from Glass Lyre Press.

Her work has received praise from Al Young, Ursula LeGuin, Dean Rader and Ellen Bass. She has been short listed for the Muriel Craft Bailey awards (Comstock Review) Lois Cranston Memorial Awards (Calyx), Atticus Review, and the Jack Kerouac Poetry contest. Her chapbook *And When the Sun Drops* (poems about her son with profound autism) won the Aurorean's Editor's Chapbook Award. Her first full length book *Floodwater* was released by Glass Lyre Press in 2014 and won the Lyrebird award. Her second book *Prime Meridian* (also from Glass Lyre Press) was released in early 2020 and was finalist in the Best Book Awards and the 2021 International Book Award. About this book, Juan Herrera says, "We need this wisdom book, clear elixirs from the Source."

Kimberly Ann Priest is the author of *Slaughter the One Bird* (Sundress 2021), *Parrot Flower* (Glass 2021), *Still Life* (PANK 2020), and *White Goat Black Sheep* (Finishing Line Press 2018). Winner of the New American Press 2019 Heartland Poetry Prize, her work has appeared in journals such as *North Dakota Quarterly, Salamander, Slipstream, The Berkeley Poetry Review, Borderland* and many others. She is an assistant professor at Michigan State University, associate poetry editor for the *Nimrod International Journal of Prose and Poetry*, and an Embody reader for *The Maine Review*. Find her work at kimberlyannpriest.com.

Lindsey Royce's poems have appeared in American and international periodicals and anthologies, including the *Aeolian Harp Anthology* Vols. 5 and 7; *Cutthroat: A Journal of the Arts* (periodicals and anthologies); *The Dreaming Machine: Writing and Visual Arts from the World; The New York Quarterly, Poet Lore*, and *Washington Square Review*. Her poems, "The Sensual Sea" and "Adagio for Heart Strings", were nominated for Pushcart Prizes in 2019 and 2020 respectively. Royce's first poetry collection, *Bare Hands*, was published by Turning Point in September of 2016, and her second collection, *Play Me a Revolution*, published by Press 53 in September of 2019, won the silver medal for poetry in the 2020 Independent Publishers Book Awards. Currently, she is editing her third poetry collection, *The Book of John*, for publication.

Barbara Ungar has been writing poems since she was 7. Her earliest influences—Edward Lear's "Nonsense Alphabets" and "The Jumblies," Robert Browning's "The Pied Piper of Hamelin," and Laura E. Richards' "Eletelephony"—may still be detected in her most recent full-length collection, *Save Our Ship,* selected by Mark Jarman for the Snyder Prize from Ashland Poetry Press. SOS was named to Kirkus Reviews' Best Books of 2019; it also won a Franklin Award from the Independent Book Publishers Association and was a Distinguished Favorite at the Independent Press Awards.

Prior books include *Immortal Medusa*, named to *Kirkus Reviews'* Best Books of 2015, and also available as an audiobook on Audible; *Charlotte Brontë, You Ruined My Life*; and *The Origin of the Milky Way*, which won the Gival Prize and a silver Independent Publishers award. She has read widely, including at The Dodge Poetry Festival, The Poetry Society of America, and Poets House. Her work has been published in the *Southern Indiana Review, Rattle, Gargoyle, Atticus Review, Pedestal, Salmagundi, Hypertext*, and many other journals. A professor at the College of Saint Rose in Albany, NY, she lives in Saratoga Springs. www.barbaraungar.net.

Alexandrine Vo (b. 1986) grew up in Quang Nam Province, Vietnam. A Gates Scholar, she earned BA degrees in literature and philosophy from Baylor University, an MA in English Literature from the University of Washington, and an MFA in Creative Writing from Boston University where she was a Robert Pinsky Global Fellow and a George Starbuck Fellow.

Her poems have been published in England, Ireland, France, and the U.S., appearing in *Salamander, Poetry Ireland Review, Popshop Magazine, Painted Bride Quarterly, Bellevue Literary Review, CALYX, The Bitter Oleander, Fjords Review, The Carolina Quarterly,* and *The American Poetry Review*, among others. Alexandrine is the Featured Poet in *The Stinging Fly's* Winter 2013-14 issue. Her work has been nominated for the Pushcart Prize and Best New Poets 2018.

She has completed a first full-length collection, *As Though We Are One*, which was named Finalist for the 2015 Kundiman Poetry Prize, and is currently at work on her second collection, *The Gallant South*. For more information, visit maythefirst.net.

Jeanne Wagner is a retired tax accountant. She was born in San Francisco and grew up in Sacramento. She graduated from University of California, Berkeley with a degree in German and has a M. A. in Humanities from San Francisco State University. She lives with her husband, Bill, dog Gretchen (the inspiration for "Dogs That Look Like Wolves,") and two cats. She likes to travel, read mysteries, play backgammon, and watch foreign mysteries and classic films. Jeanne is the author of four chapbooks and three full-length collections: *The Zen Piano Mover* from NFSPS Press, 2004 winner of the Stevens Manuscript Award; *In the Body of Our Lives*, released by Sixteen Rivers Press in 2010 and *Everything Turns Into Something Else*, runner-up for the Grayson Books Prize. Her work has appeared in *Alaska Review, Cincinnati Review, North American Review, River Styx, Southern Review, Poetry Daily, Verse Daily* and Ted Kooser's *American Life in Poetry*.

Martin Willitts Jr is a retired Librarian living in Syracuse, New York. He was nominated for 15 Pushcart and 13 Best of the Net awards. Winner of the 2012 *Big River Poetry Review's* William K. Hathaway Award; 2013 Bill Holm Witness Poetry Contest; 2014 Broadsided award; 2014 Dylan Thomas International Poetry Contest; *Rattle* Ekphrastic Challenge, June 2015, Editor's Choice; *Rattle* Ekphrastic Challenge, Artist's Choice, November 2016, Stephen A. DiBiase Poetry Prize, 2018; Editor's Choice, *Rattle* Ekphrastic Challenge, December, 2020. He won a Central New York Individual Artist Award and provided "Poetry on The Bus" which had 48 poems in local buses including 20 bi-lingual poems from 7 different languages.

Martin Willitts Jr has 25 chapbooks including the *Turtle Island Quarterly* Editor's Choice Award-winning *The Wire Fence Holding Back the World* (Flowstone Press, 2017), plus 21 full-length collections including the Blue Light Award 2019, *The Temporary World*. His new full-length is *Harvest Time* (Deerbrook Press, 2021). Forthcoming books include *Not Only the Extraordinary are Exiting the Dream World* (Flowstone Press, 2021), "All Wars Are the Same War" (FutureCycle Press, 2022).

He is an editor for the *Comstock Review* and Judge for the New York State Fair Poetry Contest.

Glass Lyre Press

exceptional works to replenish the spirit

Glass Lyre Press is an independent literary publisher interested in technically accomplished, stylistically distinct, and original work. Glass Lyre seeks diverse writers that possess a dynamic aesthetic and an ability to emotionally and intellectually engage a wide audience of readers.

Glass Lyre's vision is to connect the world through language and art. We hope to expand the scope of poetry and short fiction for the general reader through exceptionally well-written books, which evoke emotion, provide insight, and resonate with the human spirit.

Poetry Collections
Poetry Chapbooks
Select Short & Flash Fiction
Anthologies

www.GlassLyrePress.com

www.ingramcontent.com/pod-product-compliance
Lightning Source LLC
Chambersburg PA
CBHW030155100526
44592CB00009B/287